Cambridge Experience Readers

SP

Please return/renew this item by the last date shown
on this label, or on your self-service receipt.

To renew this item, visit **www.librarieswest.org.uk**
or contact your library

Your borrower number and PIN are required.

CAMBRII

D1350128

4 4 0067587 5

CAMBRIDGE
UNIVERSITY PRESS

University Printing House, Cambridge CB2 8BS, United Kingdom

One Liberty Plaza, 20th Floor, New York, NY 10006, USA

477 Williamstown Road, Port Melbourne, VIC 3207, Australia

314–321, 3rd Floor, Plot 3, Splendor Forum, Jasola District Centre, New Delhi – 110025, India

79 Anson Road, #06–04/06, Singapore 079906

Cambridge University Press is part of the University of Cambridge.

It furthers the University's mission by disseminating knowledge in the pursuit of education, learning and research at the highest international levels of excellence.

www.cambridge.org

© Cambridge University Press 2014

First published 2014
Reprinted 2018

Margaret Johnson has asserted her right to be identified as the Author of the Work in accordance with the Copyright, Design and Patents Act 1988.

Printed in Italy by Rotolito S.p.A.

ISBN 978-11-0769-061-5 Paperback; legal deposit: M-7295-2014

No character in this work is based on any person living or dead. Any resemblance to an actual person or situation is purely accidental.

Illustrations by José Rubio
Audio recordings by BraveArts
Cover image by Superstock
Typeset by Oscar Latorre

Contents

People in the story

Kieran: a twelve-year-old boy
Mum: Kieran's mother
Dad: Kieran's father
Fred: Kieran's pet spider, a Chilean Rose tarantula
Connor O'Brien: a boy in Kieran's class
Mrs O'Brien: Connor's mother
Mr Robins: Kieran's science teacher
Miss Burton: Kieran's geography teacher

BEFORE YOU READ

1 Look at the pictures in Chapter 1. What do you think?
Answer the questions.

1 Who is climbing the building?

....

2 Who does Kieran talk to in his room?

....

Christmas lights

'Twenty seconds to go, everybody!' said the DJ[1].

I was outside Sheffield Town Hall. Sheffield is a big city with lots of people, and thousands were there to see the Christmas lights[2] go on. My Dad was with me, but he said he had to do something. That was fifteen minutes ago.

'Where are you, Dad?' I thought. 'You're not going to see the lights go on!'

Then the DJ said, 'OK, everybody! Ten, nine, eight, seven, six …' We all said the numbers with him.

'… five, four, three, two, one!'

The Christmas lights went on all over the buildings. They were beautiful. Everyone said, 'Ah!' or 'Ooh!' And we all looked up at them.

That's when I saw Dad. He was on the side of the Town Hall. 'He's climbing up!' I thought. 'Oh no! Turn the lights off! Turn them off!' I didn't want people to see him.

But it was too late. 'Wow!' said the DJ. 'Look, everybody! Someone's climbing up the Town Hall!'

People said 'Ah' and 'Ooh' again, but this time they were afraid. Dad looked very small up there.

'Is he going to fall[3]?' the woman next to me said. 'I can't look!'

I didn't want to look. But I had to. Because that was my dad up there!

Dad went slowly up the building. He loves climbing and he knows what he's doing. But the building was very tall and there were lots of people. He stopped to look at us. 'Think about what you're doing, Dad!' I told him in my head. That's what he always said to me when we went climbing. 'Think about what you're doing, Kieran!'

Dad started climbing again. After five minutes he got to the top.

7

'How about that, everybody?' the DJ said. 'Make some noise for the climber!'

Everyone shouted and called out. But I didn't. I saw two policemen – they were going into the Town Hall.

'What are they going to do?' I thought.

After five minutes, the policemen came out again – with Dad. They took him away, and he shouted over to me: 'Go home, Kieran. Mum finishes work at nine o'clock.'

'That's his son!' the woman next to me said. Then everyone looked at me. I wanted to die.

*   *   *

Mum wasn't back from work when I got home. I went up to my bedroom and told Fred all about Dad. Fred's my pet[4] spider. I tell him everything.

'Why did he climb up there, Fred?' I asked. 'Why?'

Fred walked over my hand. He wanted his dinner.

'The TV people were there!' I told Fred. 'Now everyone at school is going to know about it. Connor O'Brien is going to know about it!'

Fred walked up my arm. I knew he understood. I also knew he was hungry. I put him back in his home and gave him his food. I watched him eat. After a minute, I put my computer on and started to write. I write something every day – about spiders or about how I feel.

Young spiders aren't very easy to see. This is because they don't have much colour. I want to be a young spider. I don't want people to see me.

LOOKING BACK

• •

1 Check your answers to *Before you read* on page 4.

ACTIVITIES

• •

2 Complete the sentences with *Kieran, Dad* or *Fred*.

1 ___Kieran___ is outside the Town Hall.

2 _____ is watching the Christmas lights go on.

3 _____ is climbing up the Town Hall.

4 _____ tells _____ everything.

5 _____ is hungry.

6 _____ writes something every day.

3 <u>Underline</u> the correct words in each sentence.

1 The Christmas lights go *on / off* all over the buildings.

2 Kieran *wants / doesn't want* people to see Dad.

3 Kieran *watches / doesn't watch* Dad climb the Town Hall.

4 Dad climbs *quickly / slowly* up the building.

5 The Town Hall is *tall / not very tall*.

6 Kieran is *happy / unhappy* about Dad.

7 Mum *is / isn't* at home when Kieran gets home.

8 *No one / Everyone* at school is going to know about Kieran's dad.

4 Match the questions with the answers.

1 Why was Kieran outside the Town Hall? [6]
2 Who goes into the Town Hall? ☐
3 Who does Kieran talk to when he gets home? ☐
4 What does Kieran write about? ☐

a Fred, his pet tarantula.
b He was watching the Christmas lights go on.
c About spiders or the way he feels.
d Two policemen.

5 Who or what do the underlined words refer to?

> the DJ   Dad (x2)   the Christmas lights
> the policemen (x2)   Fred (x2)

1 We all said the numbers with <u>him</u>. *the DJ*
2 I didn't want people to see <u>him</u>. ....
3 And we all looked up at <u>them</u>. ....
4 'Is <u>he</u> going to fall?' ....
5 'What are <u>they</u> going to do?' ....
6 <u>They</u> took him away. ....
7 I knew <u>he</u> understood. ....
8 I watched <u>him</u> eat. ....

LOOKING FORWARD

6 Tick (✓) the things you think are true in Chapters 2 and 3.

1 Connor O'Brien says bad things to Kieran at school. ☐
2 Dad tells Kieran he's sorry. ☐

Chapter 2

At school

The next day was a Friday. On the bus to school, I sat near a man with a newspaper.

'Listen to this,' the man said to his wife. 'David Riches, 42, is going to lose his job next week. Mr Riches said, "I love my work. I don't want to finish. I wanted to climb the Town Hall because I'm not happy about losing my job. I'm sad and I wanted everyone to know about it."'

The man with the newspaper looked angry. 'Stupid man!' he said. 'When I lost my job I didn't climb the Town Hall! I just got another job.'

'He didn't think about his family when he went up there,' said his wife. 'It was a stupid thing to do.'

I looked out of the window.

When I got to school, Connor O'Brien laughed at me. 'Hey, Kieran!' he shouted. 'Does your dad think he's a spider?' And he made a spider with one hand and a building with the other hand.

My face went red.

'If your dad's a spider, and you're his son, then you're Spider Boy!' Connor laughed.

Just then, Mr Robins, the science teacher came in. 'Did I hear you say "spider"?' he said. 'Well, that's good, because we're going to learn about spiders today.'

We all sat down and the lesson started. It was very interesting. But it wasn't easy to listen. Every few minutes Connor looked at me and made his hand climb like a spider.

At the end[5] of the lesson, Mr Robins told us about our homework. 'I want you to find out about spiders that live in the UK. You can use books and the internet. But try to find some live spiders to look at, too. Next week you can all speak to the class about what you learned.'

'Hey, Spider Boy!' Connor said to me. 'Are you going to climb up the school building at lunch time?'

'No!' I said. I was angry now, and Mr Robins looked over at us.

'Connor, Kieran,' he said. 'Because you two like talking so much, you can work together[6] on your homework.'

'Me and Connor, work together?' I thought. 'Oh no!'

Baby Australian Crab spiders eat their mothers. Mother Australian Crab spiders are food for their babies. I know just how those mothers must feel at lunch time. Afraid. Very afraid.

Chapter 3

Talking to Mum

When Mum isn't working at nights, she meets me from school. That Friday, when I got into the car, she asked me about my day. She often asks me about my day. Sometimes she listens, and sometimes she's still thinking about work. Mum's a nurse at Sheffield hospital⁷. She loves her job.

'We learned about spiders in science today,' I told her.

She smiled. 'You know a lot about spiders anyway!' she said.

Then I said, 'Mr Robins told me to do my homework with Connor O'Brien this weekend.'

Mum just said, 'Connor. That's good. You like him.'

'What?' I thought. 'Don't you know anything?'

At school, the teachers all liked me and my work was good. I never spoke to Mum and Dad about Connor and his friends – about the things they said to me. So Mum and Dad thought everything was OK.

But it wasn't.

'About what Dad did last night …' Mum said then, and I looked at her. 'I'm sorry you were there to see it.'

I looked away. 'I was afraid,' I told her. 'I thought he was going to fall.'

'I know,' Mum said. Then we had to stop at a red light, and she looked at me.

'But try to understand, Kieran. Your dad's very sad about losing his job at the factory[8]. He started working there twenty years ago.'

'Is he going to find another job?' I asked.

Mum smiled, but she looked tired. 'Yes, of course!' she said. The lights changed. Mum drove on.

'Is he going to do it again?' I asked. 'Is he going to climb another building?'

'I don't think so,' Mum said. Then she smiled. 'Anyway. Try not to think about it. Come on. I need to get something for dinner.' And she stopped at a shop.

I went into the shop with her and we got a pizza. Then Mum saw someone she knew.

'That's Mary O'Brien,' she said. 'Connor's mum.' And she called over to her. There was no time for me to say 'No!'

'Mary?' Mum said. 'I thought it was you! Kieran just said that he and Connor need to do some school work together. Do you want to bring Connor to our house at the weekend? The boys can do their homework, and we can have a cup of coffee.'

Mrs O'Brien smiled. 'Yes, we aren't doing anything on Sunday,' she said. 'Is the afternoon OK?'

'No! No! No!' I thought.

But Mum smiled back. 'Sunday afternoon is good for us,' she said.

You can die if a Sydney funnel-web spider bites[9] you. But funnel-web spiders are still much nicer than Connor O'Brien.

LOOKING BACK

1 Check your answers to *Looking forward* on page 11.

ACTIVITIES

2 <u>Underline</u> the correct words in each sentence.

1 There is a story in the newspaper about <u>*Dad*</u> / *the Christmas lights*.

2 Dad is *happy* / *sad* about losing his job.

3 Kieran thinks spiders are *interesting* / *boring*.

4 Kieran *wants* / *doesn't want* to do his homework with Connor.

5 Mum *never* / *sometimes* listens to Kieran.

6 Dad started working at the factory *two* / *twenty* years ago.

7 Mum and Kieran go into a shop to buy a *pizza* / *newspaper*.

3 Put the sentences in order.

1 Kieran and Mum go shopping. ☐

2 Mum asks Connor and his mum to their house on Sunday. ☐

3 Kieran hears a man talking about Dad. ☐1☐

4 Kieran has a science lesson about spiders. ☐

5 Kieran and Mum talk about Dad. ☐

6 Connor calls Kieran 'Spider Boy'. ☐

4 Are the sentences true (T) or false (F)?

1 The man on the bus thinks Dad was right to climb the Town Hall. ☐ F

2 Mum and Dad think Kieran is happy at school. ☐

3 Kieran wants Dad to climb another building. ☐

4 Kieran goes home from school on the bus. ☐

5 Mum sometimes works nights. ☐

6 Kieran doesn't do very well at school. ☐

7 Kieran doesn't tell Mum and Dad everything about school. ☐

8 Kieran wants Connor to come to his house at the weekend. ☐

5 Answer the questions.

1 What does Connor call Kieran at school?

....

2 What does Kieran have to do for homework?

....

3 Why doesn't Mum always listen to Kieran?

....

4 Why do Mum and Dad think everything is OK at school?

....

5 Why was Kieran afraid when Dad climbed the Town Hall?

....

6 Tick (✓) the things you think are true in Chapters 4, 5 and 6.

1 Kieran tells Dad about Connor. ☐

2 Connor comes round to Kieran's house. ☐

3 Kieran and Connor do their homework together. ☐

Chapter 4

Saturday with Dad

It was Saturday morning. Dad and I always go to the climbing wall in the city on Saturday mornings. Dad wants me to learn to climb – he thinks climbing is the best thing in the world.

'Is it this Monday you're going out for the day with the school, son?' Dad asked. 'The Peak District, isn't it?'

'Yes,' I said. I love the Peak District. It's a very big National Park with lots of hills and rocks[10], and it's only twenty minutes from Sheffield by car.

'There's a lot of good climbing in the Peak District,' Dad said.

'We're going to study rocks,' I told him. 'We're not going climbing.'

'Climbing is a great way to study rocks,' Dad said.

I didn't answer. My hands were tired. My arms were tired. Everything was tired. Climbing wasn't easy. It was like work. I wanted to be at home with a good book.

'To the right!' Dad called up to me. 'Put your hand over to the right! No, not that far! Think about what you're doing, Kieran!'

'Don't talk to me then!' I wanted to shout, but I didn't.

Somebody came to speak to Dad. I didn't want to look down, but I heard what they said.

'I saw you on TV the other night, David! When you climbed up the Town Hall! You're famous!'

'Thanks,' said Dad. 'I enjoyed it. I want to climb St Paul's Tower next!'

'St Paul's Tower!' I thought. 'That's very tall!'

'Kieran!' Dad shouted at me. 'Look where your foot's going!'

But it was too late. I fell.

After the climbing, we went to the café. 'You can try again next Saturday,' Dad told me.

I didn't say anything. There were a lot of things I never said.

'I hate climbing!'

'I don't enjoy school!'

'I don't like Connor O'Brien!'

'You never listen to me!'

'You find a table,' Dad said. 'I'm going to get some drinks. Hot chocolate all right?'

'OK,' I said.

Spiders need to drink. That's why you find them in your bath. But when a spider's in a bath, it can't climb out again. It tries and it tries, but it just can't do it.

Chapter 5

Sunday with Connor

On Sunday afternoon, Connor arrived at our house with his mum.

'Take Connor up to your room, Kieran,' Mum said.

She took Mrs O'Brien into the kitchen to make her a cup of coffee. And I was alone with Connor.

I didn't want to be with Connor, and I knew he didn't want to be with me. But we had our schoolwork to do. I said, 'My room's … er … up here.' And I started to go up.

Connor didn't speak, but I heard him coming after me. Then we were in my room, just the two of us. It didn't feel right. Connor said bad things to me, and about me, every day. And now he was here, in my room!

Connor is a big boy, and my room is small. It has lots of things in it – books, pictures, old toys. I put the computer on.

'Did you make this?' asked Connor.

I looked and saw he had my toy plane. 'Yes,' I said. 'I made it when I was eight.'

'Ah,' said Connor and he laughed at me. Then he put the plane down and looked for something new to laugh about.

I said quickly, 'I've got some books on spiders to help us with our homework.' Connor didn't look at me.

'Homework is stupid,' he said.

'Well, there's Fred too,' I said. 'Do you want to meet him?'

Now Connor looked at me. 'Who's Fred?' he asked.

I went over to Fred's house. 'He's a spider,' I said. 'A Chilean Rose tarantula. He's two years old. Come and look.' I called to Fred. 'Fred! Someone's here to meet you!'

But Connor didn't move. When I looked at him, I saw that his face was very white. I asked, 'Are you OK?'

Connor was quick to reply. 'Of course, I'm OK!' he said. 'I just think spiders are stupid, that's all.'

'Oh,' I said. I wanted to say, 'You think *everything* is stupid! But we still have our homework to do!' But I was too afraid to speak to Connor like that.

'This is boring,' said Connor. 'I'm going to get a drink.' And he got up and walked out.

I didn't try to stop him. 'You're not boring, are you?' I said to Fred. '*He's* boring!'

I waited for ten minutes, but Connor didn't come back. I went downstairs to look for him. He was in the sitting room with my Dad.

'Oh, hello, Kieran,' Dad said. 'Connor and I are just talking about climbing.'

I saw that Dad had some of his old photos out.

Connor had one of the photos in his hand. He didn't look at me. 'You climbed up here when you were my age?' he asked Dad.

Dad smiled. 'Yes,' he said. 'I climbed it with my father.' Dad started to tell the story of the climb. Because I knew the story, it wasn't very interesting to me. But Connor was very interested. His mouth was open when Dad told him how he nearly fell from the mountain.

People who live until they are eighty eat about eight spiders before they die. That's one every ten years. Spiders go into people's open mouths when they are sleeping. Spiders like open mouths.

Chapter 6

Out of school

The next day was the class visit to the Peak District for geography. Everyone was happy to be going out of school for the day.

Connor and his friends were at the back of the bus. I didn't want to sit near them, but there weren't any other places to sit. Jenny Brown came and sat next to me. I like Jenny.

The bus drove away and Miss Burton, the geography teacher, stood at the front to talk to us. 'Right, everyone,' she said. 'When we get there, Mr Parks from the Study Centre is going to tell you all about the day. We're going to be studying rocks and I think it's going to be a lot of fun[11]. But just look at the rocks, OK? Please don't climb on them. And you mustn't go off anywhere alone. Understand?'

'Yes, Miss Burton,' lots of people said. But at the back, Connor and his friends just laughed and made a lot of noise.

'What are you doing, Connor?' Miss Burton said, and she came down to the back of the bus.

Jenny had a look. 'Connor's talking about your friend Fred,' she said. 'His friends think it's very funny. Who's Fred?'

'He's my pet spider.' And I told Jenny all about Connor's visit to my home.

Jenny was very interested in Fred. 'A tarantula!' she said. 'That's nice. I've got a cat, but all she does is sleep. She's boring!'

I smiled. 'Fred sleeps in the daytime,' I told her. 'Then he wakes up in the evening.'

Jenny had lots of questions about Fred. It was good to talk about him. People aren't often interested. They don't like spiders, and they don't often want to hear about Fred.

When we got off the bus, I heard Connor behind me. 'He talks to his spider, you know,' he told Jenny. He laughed. Then he put his hands up and made them 'talk' – his left hand was me, and his right hand was Fred.

'I love you, Fred,' the left hand said. 'I love you too, Kieran. Where's my dinner?' the right hand answered. Connor's friends laughed too, and my face went red.

'Come on, everybody!' Miss Burton said. 'It's time to go into the Study Centre. Mr Parks is waiting for us!'

Connor and his friends laughed at me one more time before they went into the Study Centre.

'I don't know why he hates me so much,' I said to Jenny.

'It's not just you,' Jenny said. 'Actually, I don't think he's very happy at home.'

I looked at her. 'Don't you?'

'No,' she said. 'He lives in my road. We're at number twenty-two, and he's at number thirty-five. His dad is always shouting about something. Everyone in the street can hear him.'

'Oh,' I said. I actually started to feel sorry for Connor. My dad did stupid things like climbing buildings, but he never shouted at Mum or me.

But just then, Connor called over to me. 'Hey, Spider Boy! Is Jenny your new girlfriend?' Then he looked at Jenny. 'He's actually in love with his spider, you know!'

I didn't feel sorry for Connor after that.

Everyone knows that spiders have eight legs. But some of them have eight eyes too. And with eight eyes, they can see everything. This makes it very easy for them to find and kill their food. Connor O'Brien is like a spider with eight eyes.

LOOKING BACK

1 Check your answers to *Looking forward* on page 19.

ACTIVITIES

2 <u>Underline</u> the correct words in each sentence.

1 On Saturday mornings Kieran goes to *a climbing wall* / *the Peak District*.

2 Kieran thinks climbing is *easy* / *difficult*.

3 Kieran *talks* / *doesn't talk* to Dad about school.

4 Kieran and Connor go into *the kitchen* / *Kieran's bedroom*.

5 Connor thinks Fred is *interesting* / *boring*.

6 Kieran's class go to the Peak District by *bus* / *train*.

3 Match the two parts of the sentences.

1 Kieran is going to the climbing wall again ☐ *e*

2 Connor and his mum visit Kieran's house ☐

3 Dad climbed a big mountain ☐

4 Kieran's class is going to the Peak District ☐

5 Dad was on TV ☐

a when he was twelve.

b on Sunday afternoon.

c when he climbed the Town Hall.

d on Monday.

e next Saturday.

4 Are the sentences true (*T*) or false (*F*)?

1 Dad thinks climbing is the best thing in the world. ☐ *T*
2 Kieran talks to Dad about Connor. ☐
3 Kieran and Connor start their homework. ☐
4 Connor doesn't like Kieran's toy plane. ☐
5 Connor thinks climbing is boring. ☐
6 Kieran has to sit near Connor on the bus. ☐
7 Jenny doesn't like spiders. ☐
8 Jenny lives near Connor. ☐

5 Answer the questions.

1 What are Kieran's class going to do in the Peak District?

....

2 Where does Connor go when he leaves Kieran's bedroom?

....

3 Who does Connor talk about on the bus?

....

4 Why does Kieran start to feel sorry for Connor?

....

LOOKING FORWARD
● ●

6 Tick (✓) what you think happens in the last two chapters.

1 Kieran helps Connor. ☐
2 Kieran and Connor become friends. ☐

Chapter 7

Connor's rock dance

After Mr Parks' talk, we all went out to look for rocks. We had pictures to look at and lots of questions to answer.

I was with Jenny. She read out the first thing we needed to do. 'Find a rock that looks like the rock in picture 1, and answer the questions.'

Jenny and I looked at the picture, and then up at all the rocks.

'How about that one over there?' I asked.

Jenny looked over at it, then back down at the picture. 'No, I don't think that's it,' she said. 'How about that one?'

I had a look. 'Yes,' I said. 'I think that's it. Come on.' And we started to go over.

But before we got there, somebody called to us.

'Hey! Spider Boy! Can you climb like this?'

Connor.

I looked, but I didn't know where he was. 'Can you see him?' I asked Jenny.

'Oh no! He's up there!' she said.

I looked up. And then I saw him. Up on a very big rock. 'He's climbing up!' I thought. Connor looked very small. It made me think of Dad when he climbed the Town Hall.

'What's he doing up there?' Jenny asked.

'I don't know,' I said. 'But I think we need to tell Miss Burton. You go and tell her.'

'OK,' Jenny said, and she ran off.

I went over to Connor's rock. Connor looked down at me. 'See?' he said. 'I got to the top! I'm a much better climber than you! And I don't have climbing classes every week!'

I looked at the rock. It didn't look very easy to climb. 'I'm not a good climber,' I said.

'Well, I am!' Connor smiled. He looked happy. But then his face changed. 'Get away!' he shouted. 'Get away from me!'

'Is he talking to me?' I thought.

Connor tried to get something off his trousers.

'What is it?' I thought. 'What's wrong with him?'

Then Connor started to dance on the rock. And I started to feel afraid.

'Connor!' I shouted. 'Don't do that! Sit down! You don't want to fall!'

But Connor didn't listen. 'Get them off me!' he shouted again. 'Get them off!'

'Wait there,' I said. 'I'm coming up.' I didn't know what was wrong with Connor and I didn't want to go up there. But he needed my help.

In 1973, two spiders – Arabella and Anita – went into space on Skylab 3. Were they afraid?

Chapter 8

Helping Connor

I looked at the rock. Dad taught me that, at the climbing wall. 'Look first, before you start to climb,' he always said. 'Think about where to put your hands and feet.'

I put my right foot onto the rock. Then my right hand. Above me, Connor was still saying, 'Get them off! Get them off!' I tried not to listen. I needed to think about what I was doing.

'Now your left foot, Kieran,' I heard Dad say in my head. 'And your left hand.'

I moved my left foot and my left hand. Now I was like a spider on the rock – a spider with four legs.

Suddenly I felt hot. Connor was still talking, but there was a noise in my ears. It was like being under water. 'You're going to fall,' I thought.

But then I heard Dad again. 'You can do it, son. Just take your time.'

I looked up at the rock and tried to find somewhere for my right foot. At first, I didn't think there was anywhere. Then I looked again and saw a small hole[12] in the rock. Yes, that looked OK. I moved my foot.

When I got to the top, my legs were tired. But I felt so good. 'You did it!' I thought. 'You did it!'

'Help me!' Connor shouted. And he started to dance again.

I looked at Connor's trousers and saw … spiders! Not just one or two spiders, but lots of them!

'Wow!' I said. 'I think they're wolf spiders!'

Connor did another dance. 'I'm not interested in what they are, Spider Boy!' he shouted. 'Just get them off me!'

I thought about Connor in my bedroom – about how his face went very white when I told him about Fred. 'Connor doesn't think spiders are stupid!' I thought. 'He's afraid of them!'

And I smiled. Big Connor O'Brien – afraid of spiders! I wanted to laugh, but I didn't.

'Are you two boys all right?' Miss Burton called up to us. 'Help is coming!'

'We're OK, Miss Burton!' I called back. Then I looked at Connor. 'Come on,' I said. 'Let's get these spiders off you.'

At home that evening, I told Dad all about it. He smiled at me. 'Very good, Kieran!' he said. 'I know where you were, and that rock isn't easy to climb!'

I smiled at him. 'You're a good teacher, Dad,' I said.
Dad smiled back. 'Thank you, Kieran.'
I looked at him. It was nice to see him smile. 'Why don't you do that when you finish your job?' I said.

Dad looked at me. 'Do what?'

'Teach people to climb,' I said.

'Well …' Dad started to say, but then he stopped.

'He's thinking about it,' I thought.

'I know someone who wants to learn,' I told him. 'Connor.'

'Yes,' Dad said. 'He was interested on Sunday.'

I thought about what Jenny told me – about Connor's dad. 'I don't think Connor's very happy, actually,' I said.

Dad looked at me. 'It's very kind of you to think of him, Kieran. Very kind.' He smiled at me. 'I know!' he said. 'He can come with us to the climbing wall on Saturdays!'

'Oh no!' I thought, but Dad looked very happy, and I didn't say anything.

I went up to my room to tell Fred about it. He walked up my arm. 'You can always come to the climbing wall with me, Fred,' I told him with a smile. 'If Connor isn't nice to me.' He climbed up my arm and smiled back. What? You think spiders can't smile? Of course they can!

Tarantula spiders can live for 30 years. So, look out, Connor!

LOOKING BACK

. . . .

1 Check your answers to *Looking forward* on page 33.

ACTIVITIES

. . . .

2 Put the sentences in order.

1 Kieran and Jenny start their school work. ☐ 1
2 Dad says he can teach Connor to climb. ☐
3 Kieran climbs the big rock. ☐
4 Jenny goes to tell the teacher. ☐
5 Kieran takes spiders off Connor's trousers. ☐
6 Kieran and Jenny see Connor on top of a big rock. ☐
7 Connor climbs the big rock. ☐
8 Kieran tells Dad about climbing the rock. ☐

3 Who or what do the <u>underlined</u> words refer to?

Kieran and Dad	Connor (x3)	Kieran
the spiders	Dad	Kieran and Jenny

1 'Oh no! <u>He</u>'s up there!' ...*Connor*...
2 'I think <u>we</u> need to tell Miss Burton.' ....
3 '<u>I</u>'m a much better climber than <u>you</u>.' ....
4 'Get <u>them</u> off!' ....
5 It was nice to see <u>him</u> smile. ....
6 '<u>He</u> can come with <u>us</u> to the climbing wall on Saturdays.'
   ....

4 Complete the sentences with the words in the box.

| Kieran | spiders | Connor | Jenny | ~~rocks~~ |

1 Jenny and Kieran have to answer questions about ......*rocks*...... .
2 Connor has lots of .... on his trousers.
3 .... climbs the rock to help Connor.
4 .... is afraid of spiders.
5 .... goes to get Miss Burton.

5 Match the two parts of the sentences.
1 Connor is dancing on the rock ☐*e*
2 Kieran climbs the rock ☐
3 Kieran feels good at the top of the rock ☐
4 Kieran wants to laugh ☐
5 Kieran thinks Dad could teach climbing ☐

a because he's a good teacher.
b because Connor is afraid of spiders.
c because Connor needs help.
d because he got to the top.
e because there is something on his trousers.

6 Answer the questions.
1 Why doesn't Kieran want to climb the rock?

   ....

2 What does Kieran think about when he is climbing the rock?

   ....

3 Why doesn't Kieran want Connor to go to the climbing wall on Saturdays?

   ....

Glossary

[1]**DJ** (page 5) *noun*   disc jockey, a person who plays music at a club/party etc.

[2]**light** (page 5) *noun*   something that helps us to see in the dark

[3]**fall** (page 7) *verb*   to move down from a higher place

[4]**pet** (page 8) *noun*   an animal you keep at home

[5]**end** (page 14) *noun*   the last part, just before something stops

[6]**together** (page 14) *adverb*   with another person

[7]**hospital** (page 15) *noun*   a place where people who are ill are looked after

[8]**factory** (page 16) *noun*   a place where things are made

[9]**bite** (page 17) *verb*   to cut something with the teeth

[10]**rock** (page 20) *noun*   a large piece of stone

[11]**fun** (page 29) *noun*   something you enjoy doing, something that makes you smile

[12]**hole** (page 39) *noun*   an opening in something